The Divorce Resource Series

Money Matters

A Teen Guide to the Economics of Divorce

Carlienne A. Frisch

THE ROSEN PUBLISHING GROUP, INC.
NEW YORK

Published in 2000 by The Rosen Publishing Group, Inc.
29 East 21st Street, New York, NY 10010

First Edition

Cataloging-in-Publication Data

Frisch, Carlienne, 1944–
    Money matters: a teen guide to the economics of divorce/
Carlienne A. Frisch.
        p. cm.— (The divorce resource series)
    Includes bibliographical references and index.
    Summary: This book, focusing on money and finances, explains
the changes that divorce brings to a family, including custody
issues, child support, living arrangements, visitation rights, and
other problems.
    ISBN 0-8239-3151-X
    1. Divorce— Juvenile literature. 2. Children of divorced
parents— Juvenile literature. [1. Divorce] I. Title. II. Series.
        306.89— dc21

Manufactured in the United States of America

Contents

Introduction

Half of the marriages in the United States end in divorce. When a marriage ends, it is upsetting for everyone. A divorce especially affects teens. You have to face this new reality at a time when your world already feels upside down.

Although this is a confusing time, you should know some basic facts. For starters, you are not to blame for your parents' divorce. Parents get a divorce for reasons that have to do with their relationship with *each other.* They may want to take their lives in different directions. They may not love each other in the same way they used to. They may have met someone else they want to be with. Some marriages end because of an adult's abuse of alcohol or other drugs,

---

When a marriage ends, it is upsetting for everyone.

or because of emotional or physical illness. Whatever your parents' reasons are, you could not have prevented them from getting a divorce.

If you think that your immediate future will be different after a divorce, you are probably right. You will likely live with one parent most of the time. You and your brothers and sisters may not live in the same place. You may have to move to a different home and change schools.

Chances are the issue of money will play a large role in these changes. You and the parent you live with will probably not have as much money to spend as before the divorce. You may have to get a job or work more hours at a job you already have. Earning money for your own expenses, such as school supplies or sports equipment, or for family expenses, such as groceries, may be a new priority.

This book will help you through the difficult changes that divorce often brings. In particular, this book will focus on money and finances. You may have many questions about what will happen to you. Divorce does not have to be a mystery to you or a frightening experience. By learning about the process of divorce, you will be better able to handle the changes that come with it.

CHAPTER 1

Changes to Expect

An Emotional Upheaval

Alysha's parents were always arguing. They argued about everything. Alysha thought things could not get any worse, but then her parents stopped arguing. They stopped talking to each other at all. That made Alysha very worried.

A week later, Alysha's mother told her and her little brother that Alysha's parents were going to get a divorce. Their father was going to live with a "girl-friend" who worked with him. Alysha and her brother were going to stay with their mother.

Alysha was angry at her father for leaving, but she felt relieved that her parents would not argue or avoid talking to each other anymore. She worried that the divorce might cause changes in her life, and she wondered how often she would see her father. "Nobody cares how I feel about this," she thought.

Jamal had always been an average student. His grades were mostly Cs, and he did not cause trouble for his teachers. When Jamal's parents split up, Jamal went to live with his grandfather because his mother was looking for a job in another city and his father did not want Jamal to live with him.

Soon Jamal was falling behind in his schoolwork. He wanted to spend every evening with his girlfriend, Tasha. He felt that Tasha was the one person who cared about him. Then Tasha's parents told Jamal that he could see her only twice a week. He began to cause trouble in school, getting into fights with other students and spreading rumors about them.

When you find out that your parents are going to get a divorce, you may feel relieved or you may feel angry. You will probably feel frightened and uncertain about your future. At times, you may feel several different emotions.

Both Alysha and Jamal are in divorce situations, but they are reacting differently. Alysha is keeping her feelings bottled up inside her, whereas Jamal is expressing his anger

Your girlfriend or boyfriend may be a good form of support when dealing with divorcing parents

in ways that get him into trouble. Both of them need help coping with their emotions. You probably will, too.

As your life changes during a divorce, the most basic thing to remember is that you need someone to confide in. Find someone you trust. It is okay to talk to friends, but you really need to tell an adult what is going on. A teacher, coach, or school counselor is a good choice. If you attend a church, synagogue, or temple, you can talk with a minister, rabbi, or other religious leader about how you feel. This person can help you out, or he or she will help you find someone else, such as a counselor or therapist, who can.

The following are some situations that you may need help dealing with:

> ✥ **You may want your parents to stay
> together or to get back together again.**

You cannot make this happen. You must accept the situation, even though it is not the way you want it to be. Instead of spending a lot of energy trying to change reality, think of ways to make it more bearable. Rather than complaining to your mom that she is never around anymore, make plans for spending an afternoon together.

> ✥ **Each of your parents is trying to sway
> your feelings against the other parent.**

Sometimes a parent will make comments such as "Your father doesn't care about anyone except himself" or "My parents told me not to marry your mother, and I should have listened to them." These comments are inappropriate. Because they are frustrated and hurt, your parents may not realize that their comments are putting you in an awkward position. One way to react to your parents is to have a response ready and to use it whenever you need to. "Look, Dad, I don't like your negative comments about Mom. I love you both. Please stop saying these things in front of me."

✤ **You feel as if no one supports you**.

If parents become preoccupied with their own feelings during a divorce, they may be unavailable to their children. This can make you feel lonely and neglected. Some teens try to make themselves feel better by looking for more attention or affection from other teens. It is normal to want comfort from others, but your needs may be more than one person can provide. Sometimes even best friends, boyfriends, or girlfriends may pull back from you or accuse you of being "clingy."

This is why it is so important to have a professional counselor or therapist to talk to. Counselors are much better equipped than friends to help you handle the changes that you are going through.

Legal Terms and What They Mean

Divorce is the legal ending of a marriage by a judge in a court. The judge must decide what happens to you and your parents' other children and to your parents' property and possessions, such as homes and cars.

Custody is the legal responsibility for the care and control of children after a divorce. A judge usually decides which parent will have custody. That parent will provide you with a home.

Sole custody means that one parent has complete responsibility for you and you live with that parent.

Joint legal custody means that both of your parents share in making important decisions about your your health (if you need surgery, for example), your education (whether you go to public or parochial school), and your welfare (when you may start dating).

Joint physical custody means that you will spend about the same amount of time living with each parent in his or her home. You may spend six months with one parent and six months with the other, which means that you may go to two different schools. Or you may spend the months when you are in school with one parent and spend summers and school holidays with the other parent. Joint physical custody and joint legal custody do not always go together.

A custodial parent is the parent with whom you live and who

has the most responsibility for you. In joint physical custody, both parents are custodial parents.

A noncustodial parent is the parent with whom you do not live. This person is usually the supporting parent. That means that he or she provides money for child support to the custodial parent.

Visitation rights are also called shared parenting or access to the child. The rules for the visits are decided by a judge. These rules give the parent who does not have custody permission to have you visit him or her. If a parent is a danger to you (addicted to alcohol or other drugs, mentally ill, or physically or sexually abusive), the judge may restrict that parent's visitation rights. In rare cases, the judge may refuse to give the parent visitation rights. If the parent's situation improves, the judge may expand or return visitation rights to that parent.

Child support is the money that the supporting parent (usually the parent with whom you do not live) must pay to the parent with whom the children live after a divorce. The money is used to help pay for your food, clothes, and other expenses.

Alimony or maintenance is the money paid by a divorced or separated man or woman to the former spouse for financial support. Some judges award alimony or maintenance to one of the two people who are divorcing.

Custody Issues

When your parents begin a divorce, you may wonder who will take care of you. This is a simple question, but the answer may take a while to figure out. Divorce is a complex legal process, and there are many factors to consider.

Part of the process is that each parent will hire an attorney, also called a lawyer. These lawyers will talk with a judge about child custody, child support, alimony or maintenance, and visitation rights.

In some states, depending on your age, you will be permitted to tell the judge which parent you want to live with. The court may assign you an advocate, a guardian *ad litem*. This person is an adult assigned by the court to speak in your best interest. The guardian *ad litem* will tell the judge what he or she thinks will be best for you. The judge's final decision may not necessarily be what you have said you want, but try to trust his or her judgment.

Moving

You may have to move because of your parents' divorce. This can mean living in a smaller house or apartment than you lived in before, or you might move to a mobile home.

Another possibility (for you and, possibly, one of your parents) is moving in with other relatives for a time. You may not want to live with your grandparents or with an aunt and uncle. At the same time, it is important for you to treat your relatives with respect. If you are unhappy, talk with your parent or your grandparents about how you feel. Tell them that you are not complaining but that you want to talk about your feelings so that you will feel better. Remember that your relatives are coping with extra people living in their home. Your parent may not like living with relatives either. He or she wants to find a place to live, too.

New School, New Friends

When your parents get a divorce, your custodial parent may move to another neighborhood or another town or city. You might want to stay where you are, or you might wish that you could stay with your other parent so you would not have to leave your friends and your school.

If you move away from your friends, you can still stay in touch by writing letters or e-mail.

There are ways you can cope with these changes. Moving does not necessarily mean that you lose your old friends; instead, you have a chance to gain new ones. You can easily stay in touch with your old friends by phone (if the calls are local), through e-mail, or by regular mail. If you visit your noncustodial parent during the summer and on holidays, you will have the chance to see your old friends.

Being in a new school can give you the confidence to try new things that you may not have thought of before. You can try out for a sport. You can join a club, such as drama or debate. Volunteering is another great way to meet people. Check out the local teen center for suggestions.

CHAPTER 2

Child Support and What It Means for You

When your parents get a divorce, you and the parent you live with will probably have less money to spend than when your parents lived together. Before your parents were divorced, they most likely shared family expenses. Now one parent's income has to cover most of the family expenses. The payment of child support is intended to help both parents share the costs of the family.

Child support is the money that your noncustodial parent must pay to your custodial parent. When your noncustodial parent makes regular child support payments, he or she is helping your custodial parent provide you with food, clothing, and a place to live. You should not feel guilty about your noncustodial parent paying child support. A judge in court has determined that it is the parent's responsibility.

Getting and Keeping Child Support

Your custodial parent can use a federal program called Title IV-D (Title Four D) to set up and collect child support. The amount of child support received is determined by several factors, such as your needs and the noncustodial parent's ability to pay.

Sometimes the person who is supposed to pay child support withholds it. That means that he or she does not pay it. Your custodial parent can use Title IV-D to collect child support. If the noncustodial parent has not made a child support payment for one month, the custodial parent can go to the Title IV-D office in the county where you live.

Title IV-D is a federal program. It is operated through each state's government. Through this program, your custodial parent can get child support from your other parent from a salary deduction or a tax refund. In some states, child support can be taken from your noncustodial parent's workers' compensation benefits or unemployment benefits. If your noncustodial parent is not working, a judge can order him or her to go to work. If your noncustodial parent has no income and cannot find a job, your custodial parent can apply for government assistance through the Human Services or Social Services office in the county where you live.

Financial Emergencies

Sometimes single-parent families cannot make ends meet. They may find themselves living at poverty level. If there is not enough money in your home for adequate food and shelter, you need to reach out for help.

The federal government offers financial assistance through your county's Human Services office. This office is listed under your county's name in your local phone book. The assistance may include food stamps, which you can use to get free food. Government assistance may also include a monthly check that your parent can decide how to spend. There are housing programs that provide low-cost rental housing as well.

If you are living in a house, apartment, or mobile home that is too small for your family or is not healthy and safe, your family may qualify for a Habitat for Humanity home. This organization of volunteers builds low-cost homes for families who are willing to work on the home as it is being built. To find out if your community has a Habitat for Humanity chapter, contact the national Habitat for Humanity office at (800) 422-4828.

Many community organizations help people who cannot meet their expenses. People who have no place to live can temporarily stay in a housing shelter. Families can get free food from a community food shelf. There are also programs that provide clothing to families in poverty. Look in your local phone book under "Salvation Army," "food shelves," and "homeless shelters." Also, the people who answer the phone at church offices can usually tell you where to find help.

Insurance

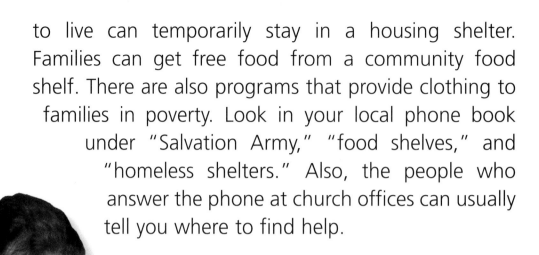

When your parents divorce, you will probably still be covered by one parent's medical insurance. This insurance pays for certain medical costs, which may include prescriptions, eyeglasses, dental care, surgery, and other medical expenses.

If you are not covered by a parent's medical insurance, you can ask your

In financial emergencies you can contact the Salvation Army, which is listed in the yellow pages

school counselor how to apply for medical insurance through your school. You and your family may also qualify for free or reduced-cost medical care if your family income is below a certain level. Your parent can apply at your county's Human Services office.

Financial Help at School

If your family is living at poverty level, you will qualify for free breakfast and free lunch at your school. If your family's income is higher but is still below a certain level, you may qualify for breakfast and lunch at reduced cost. You can ask your school counselor to help you find out if you qualify.

Your parent may not be able to pay for you to take part in activities such as sports, cheerleading, band, drama, or speech club at school. You may qualify to take part in these activities for free or at reduced cost. Activity fees, uniforms, an instrument, and other things needed for an activity can be provided by the school. Your school counselor can help you find out if you qualify.

CHAPTER 3

Helping Out

When you live with one parent, you will probably have more responsibilities than you had in the past. In this chapter you will learn more about helping out.

Set Priorities

The meaning of "helping out" will differ from family to family. You may need to do things that you have not had to before. These may include:

- Cleaning the house, dusting, vacuuming
- Doing laundry
- Baby-sitting younger siblings

❖ Cooking

❖ Doing errands such as grocery shopping

❖ Getting a job (more about this in chapter 4)

Sit down with your parent and figure out the best ways for you to contribute to the household. You may be better at some things than others; you may be a better cook than a baby-sitter, for example. If you have siblings that are old enough to help, you can figure out how to split the chores among you.

You and Your Parents

Another way you can help your mom or dad is to try hard to keep the lines of communication open. Your parent may be upset about money, tired from work, or sad about the divorce. It is important to listen when a parent wants to talk. You do not

Cooking, every once in a while, may be one way to "help your family out"

Get Organized

The best way to handle your responsibilities is to be organized. You should not try to keep your schedule in your head. Instead, buy a calendar-planner and write everything in it: after-school activities such as sports or speech club, work schedule, and the time you plan to do your homework. You should also include time to spend with your friends. You will easily see where two activities conflict. Then you may be able to make changes so that you can do both things.

have to feel disloyal to one parent when you listen to the other one. At the same time, be honest with your parents about your own feelings and share what is on your mind.

Just remember: Although sharing problems and concerns is a good thing, you cannot be expected to solve problems—especially your parents' problems—all by yourself. If you feel overwhelmed, tell your parents. Many families find that they need help handling their complicated feelings. Talking to a counselor or therapist, either alone or together, is a wise choice for families in transition.

When Anne's mother began working two jobs, Anne could not spend time with friends after school. She hurried home every day so that she would be there before Brandon, her eight-year-old brother, came home. Anne made sure she had supper ready when her mother came home between jobs. After her mother left for work at the supermarket, Anne began doing her homework. She was often interrupted because Brandon needed help with his homework. When her friends called to invite her to a movie, Anne did not go because she needed to finish her homework. She also knew that her friends would not want Brandon tagging along.

On Saturday mornings, Anne began cleaning their apartment while her mother and brother went out to do the laundry. At least, Anne thought, they did not have to make a weekly shopping trip, since her mother bought groceries a couple times a week where she worked. On Saturday afternoons and Sundays, Anne's mother tried to plan fun activities for the family. She planned things that did not cost much money, like picnics in the park. Sometimes, though, Anne and her mother were too tired to have much fun.

Anne finally made a suggestion at a family meeting. "I don't like being responsible for Brandon and for making supper every evening. I would rather work at Burger House and have you quit your evening job," she told her mother. Anne and her mother looked over the

household budget and decided to make a change. Now, Anne does her homework after school. If she wants to spend time with a friend or go to a club meeting after school, Brandon walks to his grandmother's house, where his mother picks him up after work. Their mother comes home at 5 PM, cooks supper, and is home during the evening to help Brandon with his homework. Anne works at Burger House two evenings a week and all day on Saturday. She helps her mother clean the apartment on Sunday afternoon. They are all happy with the new arrangement. Anne works hard, but she also feels independent.

It can be difficult for teenagers with the responsibility of babysitting a younger sibling to make time for homework or friends.

CHAPTER 4

Work (and Play)

Depending on your family's financial situation, you may need to get a job or work more hours at your current job. It is likely that money is tighter than it was before. You may have to buy yourself things that your parents used to buy for you, such as clothes and CDs. There is also a chance that you may have to contribute a portion of your paycheck to help meet household expenses. In cases like this, planning is key.

Map It Out

The best way to figure out money matters is to devise a budget. Find out how much money you take home on average each month. If you work a set number of hours each week—in a store, for example—add up your pay stubs. If you work as a babysitter or at another kind of job in which the hours are not regular, estimate how much you make based on what you made each month for the past few months. (If you took our advice and used that calendar-planner, this should help you remember.)

Once you know about how much money you make each month, subtract your necessary monthly expenses, such as car payments, insurance payments, or tuition bills. Also subtract incidentals, such as gas. Set aside a small amount for snacks and entertainment. Then put away a certain amount of money each week for savings. Open a savings account at a local bank. (Even if you are strapped for cash right now and can set aside only $20 each month, having a savings account is incredibly important. It is one of the smartest things you can do for your future!)

Subtract all of these things from your monthly income. How much money do you have left? This would be a good time to talk with your parent about your family's needs. If your parent needs your help meeting expenses, you should talk about exactly how much you will have to contribute and what the money will be used for.

It is possible that you may have to contribute more money than what your budget allows right now. In this case, you have two options: Cut down on your extra expenses, such as CDs or trendy clothes, or work a few more hours each week.

Be careful, however, that the needs of the family are not overwhelming your own needs. No teen should work more than twenty hours a week. Any more than this can make you slip in school or miss out on being with your friends. If your family is in deep financial need, talk to your school counselor about what is going on. He or she can help you figure out what to do from there.

Contributing to your family is a good thing, but it should never get in the way of your own life. It is possible to work *and* play.

Applying for a Job

You may want to work—but what if you have never had a job before? How do you find one?

The first thing to figure out is where to look. Some teens find jobs by calling or visiting the places they would like to work. You may hear about a job from your friends or from someone in your family. You may see a Help Wanted sign. You may also see a list of part-time jobs posted at your school's counseling office.

Be careful that the financial needs of the family are not overwhelming your own needs.

You may not be old enough to work in a fast-food restaurant, store, or office. Until you are old enough for such jobs, you can earn money by mowing lawns, baby-sitting, or taking care of people's pets. Ask your parent for advice on earning money.

When you apply for a job, the employer will ask you to prove that you are old enough to work. He or she will also ask you to prove that you are a U.S. citizen. You can provide this information by showing the employer your birth certificate, a hospital record of your birth made before you reached age five, or a religious record made before you were three months old. You also need to have a Social Security card. If you do not have a Social Security card or you cannot find your card, you should contact your local Social Security Administration office. It is listed in your local phone book under "U.S. Government."

If you are not a U.S. citizen, the employer will ask to see proof that you have permission to work in the United States. You must show the employer one of several forms issued to you by the U.S. Immigration and Naturalization Service (INS). These include Form I-551, I-94, I-688B, and I-766.

The employer will also ask you for another form of identification. You may show your driver's license,

Babysitting is a great way for young people to earn money.

passport, adoption record, school identification card, insurance policy, or some other official form.

Felicia's parents are divorced. Felicia and her two older sisters live with their mother. Her sisters both have jobs. They use their money for "extras" their mother cannot buy for them. Felicia has decided that she needs a part-time job, too. Her sister told her about a Help Wanted sign she saw at a dry cleaner's business.

Felicia called the dry cleaner and learned that he wanted someone to work six hours every Saturday. She made an appointment to apply for the job. One of Felicia's sisters told her how to get ready for the appointment. Felicia made sure that she had her Social Security card, a copy of her birth certificate, and her school identification card with her photo on it. She also called several people to ask if she could list them as references. They were people who knew her well and would speak favorably about her.

At the dry cleaner's, Felicia introduced herself and shook hands with the owner, Mr. Lambert. She asked exactly what kind of work the job involved. She learned that the person Mr. Lambert hired would work at the counter. This person would take in dry-cleaning orders and would give customers the clothes that had been dry-cleaned. Felicia told Mr. Lambert that she wanted to apply for the job.

Felicia filled out a job application. She began with her name and address. She printed the information neatly and made sure she filled in every line. Felicia listed the names and phone numbers of three refer-ences. She included a neighbor for whom she baby-sat and the parents of two friends.

Felicia gave the completed application to Mr. Lambert. She told him that she could start work next Saturday. He looked over the appli-cation and told her

Calling different buisnesses in your area is a good way to apply for a job

that he would let her know if she had the job. A couple of days later, Mr. Lambert called. He told Felicia that she should be at work at 9 AM on Saturday. She thanked him. Then she made notes on the Saturday pages in her calendar-planner.

CHAPTER 5

Love and Money

Can't Buy Me Love

Kate lives with her mother and stepfather and her two young half sisters. The family lives on a strict budget. When Kate was invited to her high school prom, her mother suggested looking in thrift stores for a prom dress. Kate asked her father for a new dress. He said, "I'll buy the prom dress for you, but I want you to think about coming to live with me. I can give you the things you want. You are old enough to make up your own mind about this. Think about it." Kate feels confused. Although she would like a new prom dress, she wants to stay with her mother and stepfather. And she does not want to disappoint her father.

Brian lives with his mother and two younger sisters. His mother has an old car. She cannot afford to buy a car and car insurance for Brian. He also cannot afford a car. The money from his part-time job goes for cool clothes and tickets to sporting events. Brian gets rides from his friends, even on dates. His girlfriend wants to know why they cannot go anywhere on their own. Brian's father offered to buy him a car.

"A guy needs a car," his father said. "Your mother doesn't understand. She just knows how to raise girls." That made Brian angry at his father. His mother works hard to be a good parent to all of her children. Brian also knows that his father wants him to move in with him and his new wife, Jane. Brian wonders what it would be like to live with his father and stepmother and to have a car. Like Kate, Brian is old enough to tell a judge that he wants to live with his noncustodial parent. He is not sure what he wants to do.

When Stacia's parents were divorced, her mother moved out. Stacia stayed with her father. He remarried, and Stacia gets along well with her stepmother. She thinks, though, that her father and stepmother are too strict. When she asks for something, *they often tell her, "We don't want you to have that, Stacia, because we don't want you to be spoiled." Stacia does not see her mother, but she visits her grandmother once a month. Stacia's grandmother buys her anything she wants. Every summer, Stacia and her grandmother spend two weeks at a vacation resort. Stacia likes the way her grandmother treats her, but sometimes she feels disloyal to her father and step-mother. They do not approve of the way Stacia's grand-mother "spoils" her. But they do not say anything because they realize that Stacia's grandmother is trying to make up for Stacia's mother leaving her. Sometimes Stacia feels guilty. She feels as though she is taking advantage of her grandmother. Stacia knows that her grandmother would like her to visit more often, but Stacia wants to spend most weekends with her friends or her family.*

How will you feel if one of your parents, stepparents, or grandparents wants to buy you costly gifts, take you on expensive vacations or frequent weekend trips, or pay for something else your custodial parent cannot afford? You may feel torn in two directions. You probably want what you are being offered, especially if your friends have it too. You may also feel that the adult is trying to buy your love. You may feel angry, confused, and tempted. That is how Kate, Brian, and Stacia feel.

If you feel torn in two directions, you should talk with the parent, stepparent, or relative whose generosity makes you feel uncomfortable or confused. This is what Brian told his father:

"Dad, I really want a car, and I appreciate your offer, but I feel that you and Jane are trying to buy my love. I'm confused. I love you even when you don't get me anything, just as I love Mom. I don't want to move in with you and Jane just to have a car."

You can remind yourself that special things are attractive, but that your custodial parent provides you with necessary things every day. Most teens know that their love cannot be bought. They usually love both of their parents. They also feel affection for their grandparents and often for stepparents as well.

Kate solved her problem by borrowing a prom dress from a friend who had worn it the previous year. Like Brian, Kate told her father how she felt. He still offers to buy her things, but now he understands that she wants to stay with her mother.

Coping with Abandonment

Some teens must cope with the opposite situation: One or both parents leave.

Your noncustodial parent might buy you clothes or take you on expensive vacations that your custodial parent can't afford.

When two people get divorced, they usually feel stress. Sometimes a person going through a divorce does not want to believe that it is happening. This is called denial. The person may also be very angry with the husband or wife who wants the divorce. The person who does not want the divorce may think, "What is the point in trying?" He or she may give up on family relationships. If one or both of your parents act this way, you should not blame yourself. It is not your fault. Once your parent accepts the fact that the marriage ended in divorce, he or she may want to be a parent to you again.

If a non-custodial parent

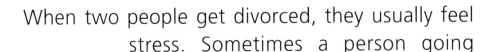

Your divorcing parents may be under a lot of stress, and may feel angry towards their former spouse

does not want a relationship with his or her children, that parent must still pay child support if the judge has ordered it. If the noncustodial parent does not pay, the custodial parent can use Title IV-D to get support.

When your parents get a divorce, you may feel that you have lost many people in your family. Sometimes grandparents, aunts, and uncles take sides with one of the parents. You and your custodial parent may not be invited to holiday celebrations or other special events.

Hector lives with his mother. His parents were divorced in the summer. At Thanksgiving, Hector and his mother ate dinner alone in their apartment. Hector wanted to be at a family dinner at his grandparents' house, like other years. But his grandparents did not want to talk to Hector's mother, so they did not invite them to dinner. Hector felt as though he had lost his grandparents when his parents got a divorce.

It is normal to feel bad when things like this happen. Talk about your feelings with your custodial parent. If you live near your grandparents, you might be able to visit them by yourself. If you do not live near them, your custodial parent may not be able to pay for you to travel to your grandparents' home. Try to talk with your grandparents. Tell them how you feel.

The next day, Hector phoned his grandparents. He told them that he felt left out. They reassured him that he would always be their grandson. They invited him to spend the next weekend with them. They told him that if he and his mother moved away, they would pay the travel costs for him to visit them.

Sometimes a custodial parent does not want his or her children because they are a reminder of the other parent. That sometimes happens when the custodial parent begins dating or gets married. The teen may be asked to live elsewhere. Although this is not the teen's fault at all, he or she has to make plans about where to move. Some teens move in with the other parent, with a grandparent, or with a friend. Sometimes the parent pays the people with whom the teen lives for expenses. In other situations, the teen's grandparents or the friend's parents pay for the teen's care.

Sometimes both parents abandon, or give up care of, their children. If you have no one to take care of you, tell your school counselor or call Human Services under your county's name in the phone book. These people will help you find out what to do.

After divorce, teens may move in with a parent, a grandparent, or a friend.

CHAPTER 6

Looking to the Future

When two single parents marry, they form a blended family, or stepfamily. When one of your parents gets married, you will become part of a blended family. If your mother marries, her husband will be your stepfather. If your father marries, his wife will be your stepmother.

There are different kinds of blended families. If your stepparent also has children, they will be your step-sisters or stepbrothers—your stepsiblings. A blended family can also be a family in which one parent has children but the other does not.

When one of your parents marries, you may have some of the same feelings you had when your parents got a divorce. You may feel resentful, angry, or sad. If your custodial parent marries, you may feel that your life is out of control. You will probably worry about changes in your family situation, and you may have new rules and responsibilities. It is normal to feel frustrated, scared, or angry. Give yourself time to adjust to these changes.

When a parent marries, you realize that your parents will not get back together. You may feel that the parent who got married is deserting your other parent. You may be angry with this parent and with your new stepparent. If your parent and stepparent have a baby, you may resent the amount of time they spend with the baby. You may feel that you are being replaced by your half sibling. It is normal to feel left out and jealous, but, blaming people or feeling angry will not change the situation.

Even if you feel good about your stepparent, you may not want him or her telling you what to do. It is normal to feel that way, but it is important to cooperate with your stepparent. Do not expect your parent always to side with you in a disagreement. You should not do things to upset your stepparent. You should also not cause arguments between your parent and stepparent or get involved in arguments between them. Suggest having a family meeting to plan your responsibilities.

Your stepparent is an important person in your parent's life. Your stepparent may also become an important person in your life. You have something in common: You and your stepfather both love your mother. You and your stepmother both love your father. You should not feel guilty if you like or grow to love a stepparent. You can love people in different ways without being disloyal.

Some teens are concerned that when a parent marries, the family will move again. Now that you are used to your new home and school, you may be worried that things will change. It is true that your family might move to a different home. There will be more money to spend on housing if two adults in your family have jobs. Your new home may be larger and nicer than where you live now. If you move, you can use the ideas for coping with a move that you read in chapter 1.

When your parent marries, you may share your home with stepsiblings. You might not like some of the changes this involves. You may have to share a room with a stepsibling. Ask for an area that is your own private space; that space can be part of a room. You should also respect other people's space. Your position in the family may change. If you are used to being the oldest or the only child, you may have to adjust to being a middle or younger child.

You may actually like some of the changes. Your stepsibling will probably be responsible for some of the chores you have been doing. You will also have someone with whom to talk, share, play games, or just hang out.

Finding Help for Problems

Some teens do not live with either of their parents. Certain parents cannot take care of their children because they have a serious, long-term illness. Some parents abuse alcohol or other drugs. If your parent cannot take care of you or your siblings, you should contact the Human Services office in your county. A social service worker will help you and your parent make arrangements for someone to take care of you.

If your parent or someone else in your family is abusing you physically or sexually, you should contact the

You may enjoy playing games and hanging out with your new stepsiblings.

Human Services office immediately. A social service worker will talk with you and your parent. This agency may begin child protection proceedings in court. A judge may place you with a responsible relative or in a foster home.

You can have an advocate represent you in court. The advocate may be a judge, a social worker, a court-appointed psychologist, or a guardian *ad litem*. You should talk with your advocate honestly about your feelings. An advocate will make a recommendation to the court that he or she believes will make you the happiest in the long run.

Foster Homes

A judge or other advocate will try to keep your family together. Sometimes, though, it may be best for you not to live with your family for a while. The judge may decide that you should live in a foster home. If you have brothers or sisters, they may be placed in the same foster home or in another one.

The adults in the home will be your foster parents. They will be responsible for you until you can return to your family. Your foster family may include other children, some of whom may be a permanent part of the family. There may also be other foster children. The foster home will have rules, just as your family does. You will be expected to follow the household rules of the foster home.

You might stay in a foster home for one or two years. Most likely, you will grow to feel like part of this family. You may find that you like your foster parents. It is not wrong or disloyal to your parents to feel that way. You are not disloyal to your parents if you get along well with your foster parents.

When you return to your family, a social worker will hold meetings to help you and your family cope with adjustments.

Emancipation

Some teens become emancipated. This means that a judge makes a court order that recognizes the teen as an adult. State laws on emancipation vary; some states do not have emancipation laws. Most teens do not become emancipated.

A teen who is emancipated is allowed to do the things an adult can do. If you are emancipated, you will be able to rent a home, borrow money, and get married. (You will not be allowed to vote until you reach voting age, however.) You will be legally responsible for your expenses, any contracts you sign, and so on.

If you live in a state with an emancipation law, you can petition the court for emancipation. The first step is

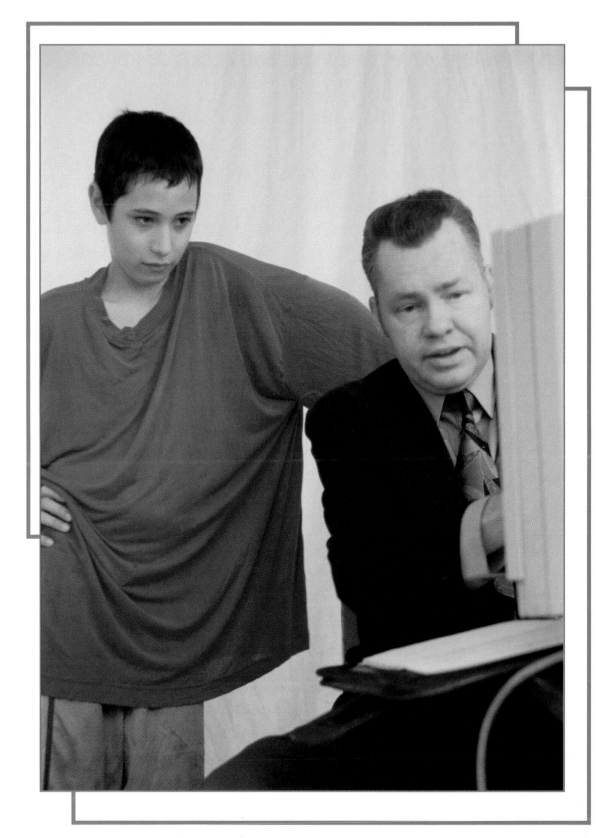

to contact your county's Human Services office. Be ready to explain why you believe that you should be emancipated. To petition the court for emancipation, you will need to get an attorney. Depending on your income, you may be eligible for free legal services. To become emancipated, you should make enough money to support yourself. If you do not, your parents may agree to provide you with financial assistance if you are emancipated.

A Final Word

The issues that surround divorce are complicated, but with the right support, you can find your way through. At the back of this book, you will find many resources that can help you—organizations, Web sites, and books like this one. Do not be afraid to ask for help when you need it. Soon you will be able to look back on this time and see how much you have learned.

To petition the court for emancipation, you will need to get an attorney.

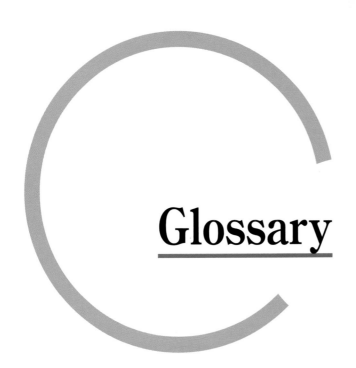

Glossary

abandonment When a parent has not had contact with his or her child for a long period of time and does not pay any child support.

abuse The deliberate harm of another person, sexually, physically, or emotionally.

alimony The money paid by a divorced or separated man or woman to the former wife or husband for financial support.

caseworker/social worker A person who helps people with their problems.

child support Money that the supporting parent must pay to the parent with whom the children live after a divorce. The money is used to help pay for the children's food, clothes, and other expenses.

custodial parent   The parent with whom the child lives and who has the most responsibility for the care of the child.

custody   Legal responsibility for care and control over children after a divorce.

divorce   The legal ending of a marriage.

emancipation   A court order made by a judge that recognizes a teen as an adult and allows the teen to do all of the things an adult can do.

foster home   A home where teens or children may live when parents or other family members cannot take care of them.

guardian *ad litem*   An adult assigned by the court to speak in the child's best interest.

joint legal custody   An arrangement in which both parents share in making substantial decisions about the care of the child.

joint physical custody   An arrangement in which the child spends about an equal amount of time with each parent in each parent's home.

noncustodial parent   The parent with whom the child does not live.

sole custody   An arrangement in which one parent has complete responsibility for the child or children.

visitation rights   The rules, usually determined by a judge, of when and how often noncustodial parents may see their children.

Where to Go for Help

In the United States

Community Information and Referral Services

(800) 352-3792

Habitat for Humanity

(800) 422-4828

Contact national organization for location of local chapter.

Jobs for America's Graduates (JAG)

1729 King Street, Suite 200

Alexandria, VA 22314

(703) 684-9479

E-mail: ars@imd-net.com

Web site: http://www.jag.org

Contact national organization for local address. Has programs for disadvantaged and at-risk students who have limited work experience and do not plan to attend college immediately after graduation or are at risk of dropping out of high school.

Parents Without Partners

420 North Michigan Avenue

Chicago, IL 60611

(800) 638-8078

(312) 644-6610

There are local chapters across the United States. The organization's International Youth Council provides support and social events for teens who live in single-parent homes.

The Stepfamily Foundation, Inc.

333 West End Avenue

New York, NY 10023

(212) 877-3244

Twenty-four-hour information line: (212) 799-STEP

Web site: http://www.stepfamily.org

WAVE

501 School Street SW, Suite 600

Washington, DC 20024

(800) 274-2005

Helps disadvantaged sixteen- to twenty-one-year-old high school dropouts and students at risk of dropping out to find unsubsidized jobs.

Youth Crisis Hotline

(800) 448-4663

In Canada

Canadian Youth Rights Association

27 Bainbridge Avenue

Nepean, ON K2G 3T1

(613) 721-1004

Web site: http://www.cyra.org

Family Service Canada

404-383 Parkdale Avenue

Ottawa, ON KIY 4R4

(613) 722-9006

Web Sites

The Kids' Corner

http://www.eros.thepark.com/volunteer/safehaven/divorce/divorce_kids.htm

For young people whose families are going through or have been through a divorce, with links to sites specifically for teens and sites in Canada.

The Kids' Page at Successful Steps

http://www.positivesteps.com/Kids.htm

Lots of information and support for kids about stepfamilies, parents, siblings, abandonment, and other subjects.

My Two Homes

http://www.mytwohomes.com/

A site where young people can order cool stuff to make life with two homes easier: a calendar to keep track of days with each parent, a handbook, a photo album, and more.

For Further Reading

American Bar Association Family Law Section. *My Parents Are Getting Divorced: A Handbook for Kids*. Chicago: American Bar Association, 1996.

Erlbach, Arlene. *Everything You Need to Know If Your Family Is on Welfare.* New York: The Rosen Publishing Group, 1998.

Frisch, Carlienne A. *Everything You Need to Know About Getting a Job*. New York: The Rosen Publishing Group, 1999.

Johnson, Linda Carlson. *Everything You Need to Know About Your Parents' Divorce*. New York: The Rosen Publishing Group, 1998.

Joselow, Beth B., and Thea Joselow. *When Divorce Hits Home: Keeping It Together When Your Family Comes Apart*. New York: Avon Books, 1996.

Index

About the Author: Carlienne Frisch

Carlienne Frisch is a freelance Minnesota writer of books for teens and children, career profiles, business and travel articles, and historical pageants. Her non-fiction books include such diverse topics as franchising, pet care, advertising, map reading, European countries, substance abuse and author Maud Hart Lovelace. Frisch has B.S. and M.S. degrees from Minnesota State University-Mankato, where she is a mass communications instructor.

Acknowledgments/Consultants

Susan Stevens Chambers, Attorney
Chesley, Kroon, Chambers & Harvey, P.L.L.P.
Mankato, Minnesota
Sherryl Wolff, M.S. in Secondary School Counseling
Mankato, Minnesota

Photo Credits

Cover and pp. 4, 15, 20, 23, 26, 30, 32, 35, 40, 42, 45, 49, 52 by Christine Walker; p. 9 by Katherine Hsu.

Design and Layout

Michael J. Caroleo

Series Editor

Erica Smith